BRIGH

THE WEB AND THE ROCK AND YOU CAN'T GO HOME AGAIN BY THOMAS WOLFE

Intelligent Education

IP INFLUENCE PUBLISHERS

Nashville, Tennessee

BRIGHT NOTES: The Web and the Rock and You Can't Go Home Again

www.BrightNotes.com

No part of this publication may be used or reproduced in any manner whatsoever without written permission, except in the case of brief quotations in critical articles and reviews. For permissions, contact Influence Publishers http://www.influencepublishers.com.

ISBN: 978-1-645425-02-1 (Paperback)
ISBN: 978-1-645425-03-8 (eBook)

Published in accordance with the U.S. Copyright Office Orphan Works and Mass Digitization report of the register of copyrights, June 2015.

Originally published by Monarch Press.
Terence Dewsnap, 1965
2020 Edition published by Influence Publishers.

Interior design by Lapiz Digital Services. Cover Design by Thinkpen Designs.

Printed in the United States of America.

Library of Congress Cataloging-in-Publication Data forthcoming.
Names: Intelligent Education
Title: BRIGHT NOTES: The Web and the Rock and You Can't Go Home Again
Subject: STU004000 STUDY AIDS / Book Notes

CONTENTS

INTRODUCTION TO THOMAS WOLFE

Thomas Clayton Wolfe was born October 3, 1900, in Asheville, North Carolina, the youngest of seven surviving children of William Oliver and Julia Elizabeth (Westall) Wolfe. His father, a towering stonecutter of dynamic speech and action, provided an image of male force and restlessness which was to endure in the mind of Wolfe throughout his life. Although his father was a brooder who drank and upset the family by his outbursts of wrath, he also had deep resources of love for nature, for the work of his hand, and for his children; and his children, in turn, worshipped him. Mrs. Wolfe, on the other hand, although not lacking in maternal feeling, was an ambiguous figure to her youngest son. In various ways, she tried to dominate him to keep him as her baby by having him sleep in her bed and by letting his hair grow long even after he was going to school. As the same time, her dissatisfaction with her lot as wife of an unambitious drunkard and her desire for security led her into independent financial endeavors which alienated her from her husband and, to some degree, from her children, whom she ceased to attempt to understand. In 1904, she made a break with her husband, taking all of the children except the eldest daughter to St. Louis to run a boarding house for visitors to the World's Fair. When one of the children died, Mrs. Wolfe returned to her husband. But in 1906, she bought a house in Asheville and ran it as a boarding house called the Old Kentucky Home. She took all of the children except Mabel, the father's favorite, to live with her. Tom spent his youth traveling between the houses of the two parents.

PRIVATE SCHOOL

At 11, Tom left the public school to become a pupil in the private North State School when it was founded by J. M. Roberts, the principal of his grammar school. Roberts' wife, Margaret, who taught in the school, became a spiritual mother to Tom. The first person to recognize his genius, she encouraged him, at the age of 14, to begin to write, to give form in language to the yearnings that would carry him beyond the mountains that surrounded Asheville.

COLLEGE

Asheville had always represented a confinement of the spirit to Wolfe and, in adolescence, when his extreme height and awkwardness intensified his self-consciousness, he longed to escape the prison of his provincial environment. When he was preparing to attend college, he set his sights on the University of Virginia or Princeton. But his father, determined that he should prepare himself for a career in law and politics, insisted he go to the state school, the University of North Carolina at Chapel Hill. In September, 1916, gawky and green, a ready target for the clever jibes and pranks of upperclassmen he arrived on campus. After a dismal freshman year he fell in love with a summer boarder at the Old Kentucky Home-a girl already engaged to be married. To add to his unhappiness, his brother Ben was rejected by the draft because of bad lungs, and the condition of his father, who was suffering from cancer, worsened markedly.

The next year was a relatively happy one. Tom joined numerous clubs and began to write for student publications. He was beginning to earn a reputation as a campus humorist.

The spring of 1918 was marred by the death of Edmund Burdick, an Asheville boy who was Tom's roommate. And that fall-after a hellish summer in Norfolk working briefly on defense jobs and almost starving-Tom endured the tragic death of his beloved brother Ben.

In his junior year Tom's interests turned toward the drama. He enrolled in a course for playwrights in which students were required to write plays using the folk materials of the Carolina Mountains. During his senior year when the question of his future began to loom, those around him spoke vaguely of journalism. But his own inclination was to go to Harvard Graduate School to become a student of Professor George Pierce Baker in the 47 Workshop for playwrights. His mother finally agreed in the late summer of 1920 to finance him for a year, and he gained admission to Harvard.

GRADUATE SCHOOL

In the North, Wolfe sought the authority and security for which he had always longed. He paid frequent visits to his uncle Henry Westall, a former minister, now a real-estate conveyancer in Boston; perhaps he hoped to discover in Westall's reminiscences about his mother's family a sense of his own identity. He worshipped Professor Baker, in whose course he enrolled. And he submitted to the influence of Kenneth Raisbeck, the aesthetic and glitteringly polished young man who was Professor Baker's assistant.

Tom stayed at Harvard for three years, concentrating on courses in literature and drama and hungrily devouring thousands of books on a multitude of subjects. In the summer of 1923, he submitted a play to the Theatre Guild for possible performance on Broadway, but the play was returned with suggestions for revision. Much as Wolfe tried to cut and organize the play according to Theatre Guild specifications, the more sprawling it became. His gift was not for condensation but for fullness of elaboration. Despondently, he took a job teaching at the Washington Square College of New York University.

NEW YORK CITY

The following years consisted of a series of frustrated explorations and quests. When not writing plays or teaching, he would prowl the streets by night, absorbing the life and mystery of the city. And when his perplexity at the hard face of the city became too great, he would escape weekends on the trains that run northward along the Hudson River (in his mind developing the symbolic associations of the train, the river, and time), often stopping at Rhinebeck to stay at the estate of Olin Dows, a friend from Harvard, a painter whose work reflected the overprotectiveness of his life as a child of wealth. In the fall of 1924 he went to Europe, meeting Kenneth Raisbeck and two Boston girls in Paris, and falling in love with the younger. When she refused him, he became involved in a jealous feud with Raisbeck which shortly terminated their friendship. Traveling alone, he resumed his writing. He returned in September, 1925 to meet a teaching commitment. As the ship docked in New York City, he met a fellow passenger, Aline Bernstein - the Esther of his novels. Although she was 44, she was a woman of charm and beauty (and a great cook, confirming Wolfe's theory that culinary ability was a measure of sensuality), and he soon fell in love with her.

After another year of teaching at N. Y. U. and several unsuccessful attempts to sell his plays, Wolfe visited London in the summer of 1926 and there began jotting down incidents from his youth as the basis for a novel. He returned to New York and accepted an offer from Mrs. Bernstein to support him until he finished his book.

In March, 1928, he began submitting his novel to publishers. In the meantime, his relationship with Mrs. Bernstein had been deteriorating because of jealous arguments. In the summer, he tried to break with her by making a tour of Europe on his own. But he could not **refrain** from writing affectionate letters, which resulted in a reconciliation that extended their affair for one more year. It was during this trip to Europe that Wolfe had a fight with several men and a woman in a Munich beer hall that resulted in his hospitalization.

PUBLICATION

While in Europe Wolfe had received a letter from Maxwell Perkins, a Scribner's editor, expressing interest in his novel. Upon his return he worked closely with Perkins, cutting and reorganizing, until the novel was ready for publication in October, 1929. In keeping with his tendency to seek authority outside of himself, Wolfe, more than any other major American author, gave responsibility for the final condition of his novel to his editor.

The reaction to *Look Homeward, Angel* was generally favorable-although the citizens of Asheville, North Carolina, were ready to lynch Wolfe for the cruel accuracy of his portrayal.

In 1930 Wolfe went to Europe on a Guggenheim fellowship and began to write a catalogue of the memories of his life. His

London meeting with Sinclair Lewis, besides providing the basis for an **episode** in *You Can't Go Home Again,* made him feel a part of the literary community. Upon his return, working in a basement apartment in south Brooklyn, with his only close friend his editor, he produced several short stories and a large sequel to *Look Homeward, Angel,* which he thought of as one novel, but which later developed into three. When Perkins received the massive manuscript, he immediately cut it into two portions, the first one ending with Eugene's meeting with Esther (based on Aline Bernstein) on shipboard, the second dealing with the subsequent romance, and concentrated his attention on the first of these. After a year and a half of editing, cutting, disputing, the new novel, to be entitled *Of Time and the River,* was ready for publication.

But the friendship of Wolfe and Perkins had been undermined. Wolfe had begun to despise himself for needing the authority of Perkins, and eventually he transferred his spite to Perkins himself. Furthermore, Perkins was relatively conservative, resisting the young author's attempts to insert social criticism in his novels at a time when Wolfe was developing a social conscience and felt a need to express protest. Too, Wolfe was becoming uneasy about his financial relationship with Scribner's and, no doubt, he began to sense that his publisher was forcing him to conform to the needs of the trade rather than encouraging his development as an individual artist-one who did not write novels with unified plots or of the proper size. More than anything else, Wolfe probably felt that Perkins and Scribner's were trying to cut him down.

To avoid the crisis of publication, Wolfe went to Europe in the spring of 1935. In May, buoyed up by favorable reviews and critical acclaim, he made a triumphal entry into Berlin, there to spend the German royalties on the translation of his first novel.

It was characteristic of Wolfe that he make up his mind on the basis of personal experience, and, in Germany, swept off his feet by the adulation of the reading public, he was conscious only of a glorious elation and was slow to recognize the dangers of Hitlerism. Not till he returned to Germany in the summer of 1936 did he become aware of the falseness and brutality of the Nazis.

THE BREAK WITH SCRIBNER'S

After his return to America in the fall of 1936, Wolfe's conflict with Scribner's reached a crisis. Intent on proving that he could write a successful novel independently of Perkins, he began to negotiate with several publishers and, after considerable confusion, accepted an offer from Harper for his next book.

In May, 1938, Wolfe left his manuscript with Edward Aswell, a Harper editor, and, after stopping at Purdue University to give a talk, made a trip through the West. On July 4, as a celebration, he took a steamship cruise from Seattle, Washington, to Vancouver, British Columbia. On board, he met a man who became sick with a chill, and he gave the man a swig from a bottle of whiskey before he took a drink himself. He contracted a cold which led to pneumonia-which reactivated an old tubercular condition. He died of tuberculosis of the brain on September 15, 1938, a month before his thirty eighth birthday. His manuscript, put into final form by Aswell, was published as two separate novels, *The Web and the Rock* (1939) and *You Can't Go Home Again* (1940).

THE NOVELS

The pattern of Wolfe's life emerges as a quest for authority, fellowship, literary success, and identity. This quest is depicted in four novels consisting of 700-1000 pages each and in several short pieces dealing with the same or related materials. His first novel, *Look Homeward, Angel,* covers the first 20 years in the life of Eugene Gant-a fictional personality extremely close to Wolfe's own, although Eugene, it should be mentioned, is more the genius, less the ordinary boy with a sense of humor and an interest in games and sports than was Tom Wolfe. The second, *Of Time and the River,* is a sequel to the first, depicting Eugene's wanderings during the next four years. *The Web and the Rock,* his third novel, introduces a new character, George Webber: it parallels the earlier works in its treatment of the life of a boy growing up, but then goes on to narrate a major love affair which begins when he is 24. The fourth novel, *You Can't Go Home Again,* continues the experiences of George Webber from age 28 to 36.

TECHNIQUE

Although Wolfe is an autobiographical writer utilizing a remarkable memory to recapture the details of the past, his art is far from reportage. His imagination colors and heightens every detail that it fixes upon. Fitzgerald, in a letter, took him to task for his failure to select-but he does, in one sense, select: he does choose and adapt the experiences recalled from the deep well of memory. He does not "select" in the way that writers intent on the well-made novel do. He does not unify plot, character, and **theme** in the conscious manner that Fitzgerald's notes on his writings reveal that he did. But he does deal with a series of **episodes** unified by **theme** and controlled by a natural sequence of moods. Generally, too, he gives his work a tonal unity by choosing descriptions of human beings living life in an intense way-eating, drinking, arguing, loving. The imaginative world of

Wolfe is robust. It is also full of night and mystery. His world is an accumulation of vague impressions which become more profound as time goes on. Not all of his excesses are justified, but they contribute to a total dynamic view of life. For Wolfe, a life without excess of passion is no life at all. Even in the later works where satiric attitudes become strong, it is the energy of his affirmation that "the essence of religion for people of my belief, is that man's life can be, and will be, better," it is his love of life that is the most powerful element in his writing.

THEMES

The novels of Wolfe are unconventional in that they achieve unity not from the conventional plot but from symmetries of character and repetition of motifs or themes. The principal themes recur in all of the novels-although with a gradual shift in emphasis. The first **theme** is one of escape. The young boy longs to escape the confinement of the family and its parochial attitudes; when he attempts actual flights beyond the family boundaries, he encounters new impediments to his freedom. The second **theme** is one of search. The hero looks for a father, mother, or body of beliefs to which he can adhere. His search usually leads him to the earth, the source of life. The third **theme** is time, the hero seeking to define and control time in order to recapture the past. The fourth **theme**, which is less dominant in the early novels than in the later, is concerned with change; the hero is unable to achieve permanence because the world is in a constant state of flux. The four themes, which together constitute a quest for self-discovery, define a longing that is universal. But because the longing can never be satisfied in a limited world, the novels are colored with the romantic **irony** of dreams pursued but never possessed.

THE WEB AND THE ROCK

BOOK I: THE WEB AND THE ROCK

CHAPTERS 1-4

Plot Analysis

Born in 1900 (the birth date of Thomas Wolfe and Eugene Gant), George Webber grows up in the town of Libya Hill, Old Catawba. His father, who had been divorced as a young man and who deserted George's mother in 1908, was, in spite of his reputation, an attractive figure. But when his mother died shortly after her husband's desertion, George was taken from his father and brought up by his mother's gloomy eldest sister, Aunt Maw Joyner, with the aid of her brother Mark and his wife Mag Joyner. In his childhood the world is clearly divided into two camps: that of heroes like his father, or Nebraska Crane, the Cherokee boy who uses a baseball bat to defend George from a group of bullies; and that of his enemies, including the Joyner family and the young toughs from the other side of town.

Comment

In an unfinished letter to his editor Wolfe proposed that the story of George Webber should be "the adventures of what I call 'the innocent man' through life" and that it should be a novel "about discovery-about discovery not in a sudden and explosive sense as when 'some new planet breaks upon his ken,' but of discovery as through a process of finding out, and of finding out as a man has to find out, through error and through trial, and through fantasy and illusion, through falsehood and his own damn foolishness, through being mistaken and wrong and an idiot and egotistical and aspiring and hopeful and believing and confused, and pretty much, I think, what every damned one of us is and goes through and finds out about and becomes" (*Letters*, p. 711). In an Author's Note affixed to the novel, Wolfe repeats his promise that this is to be a book of discovery and goes on to state that this novel marks "a genuine spiritual and artistic change. It is the most objective novel that I have written." The objectivity is in the detached attitude with which the author often views his **protagonist**, and it is in his frequent use of **satire** at the expense of American society.

Notes: *The Web And the Rock*-Webber, maker of webs, weaves outward, from the self to the world, from the confining provincial center to a complexly textured consciousness of the whole life. He assimilates and gives form to knowledge based on his experience and seeks corroboration in the lives of contemporaries and in the past, especially of the South. The web, however, as it becomes an image in the novel, also has associations with darkness and destruction - the inhibiting influence of possessive people which, like a spider web, would thwart his freedom and the contagious poison of hatred which he is exposed to as a charity boy, a poor relation to the Joyners.

The rock is associated with the future. His college, Pine Rock, will introduce him to academic and literary challenges which begin to prepare him for the city of the North - the highly complex metropolis where he is to acquire maturity and where he hopes to discover a rock-like authority which he associates with his father, who came from the North. New York, a city of golden visions and of the pilgrim's goal, a New Jerusalem of the senses, is in reality a forest of stone, whose people and institutions suffer from hardness of heart. But that is one of George's later discoveries. For now, it is the city of promise.

Comment

"The Child Caliban" - The title implies that George Webber at the beginning of his career of discovery is as lacking in substantial form as the monster Caliban in Shakespeare's *Tempest*.

CHARACTER ANALYSES

George "Monk" Webber

The hero of Wolfe's last two novels is as sensitive and prone to dreams as Eugene Gant, but he is much more a typical American youth. As Wolfe explains the difference, "this is a book about discovery, and not about self-justification; it hopes to describe the pattern that the life of Everyman must, in general, take in its process of discovery; and although the **protagonist** should be, in his own right, an interesting person, his significance lies not in his personal uniqueness and differences, but in his personal identity to the life of every man." He uses his hero as a "polar instrument round which the events of life are grouped, by means of which they are touched, explained, and apprehended, by means of which they are seen and ordered." (*Letters,* p. 714). This explains Wolfe's tendency to generalize upon the experience of George, as at the end of Book III where he addresses a rhetorical question to the reader: "Has it been otherwise with any man?"

John Webber

George's father, "'a Northern man,' of Pennsylvania Dutch extraction," who came to Libya Hill to work as a mason and builder. He is a man of instinct and passion, as is suggested in his ape-like figure-short legs and torso and long arms. His drinking and infidelity alienate him from his wife's relatives.

Aunt Maw Joyner

A gloomy, brooding spinster, the aging sister of George's mother, who takes care of him. In a voice similar to Eliza Gant's she tells stories of the family's past, for example, of George's granduncle Rance who was both a Civil War soldier famous for his rancid smell, and a religious prophet who was frequently seen as an apparition before death.

Nebraska Crane

George's fearless friend and protector; part Cherokee, he represents an ideal of honor and individualism. Several critics have pointed to this figure as a creation of Wolfe's without an autobiographical basis, but Wolfe does say of this character, "I have got the man, I knew him as a child-he never made the big League [as does Nebraska], but he could have" (*Letters* pp. 722-723).

THE WEB AND THE ROCK

BOOK II: THE HOUND OF DARKNESS

· ·

CHAPTERS 5-9

As George matures, the varied quality of life impresses itself upon him. Chapter 7, in short story form, tells of "The Butcher," Lampley, his crude wife, sensual daughter, and confused son, Baxter, who is applauded for his sexual conquests but disowned for dishonesty. Later we realize that this chapter is an important introduction to the chain reaction of brutality. Chapter 8 examines similar destructive powers as they flare up in Dick Prosser, a Bible-reading Negro handyman who works in the home of George's friend, Randy Shepperton. Dick's athletic prowess, military manner, and knowledgeability make him a hero of the boys in the town. But one day, after drinking and arguing over a woman, he goes berserk, shooting several men before he is tracked down and killed by an illegal posse who hangs his bullet-ridden body in a funeral parlor window. Chapter 9 describes the journeys of George and his uncle into the mountains above the town where the man would scream out in hatred against his father and his wife.

Comment

Locust Street, the street on which George lives, is aptly named because in later years its memories will swarm out at the author, evoking a consciousness of the "buried life" which lies beneath the world of sense. Mostly they are memories of a destructive power associated with that part of his "web" of experience dominated by the Joyners. The butcher and his family, Dick Prosser, and Uncle Mark represent a violence which is part of the world and George's experience of the world, and which he must attempt to extirpate. These brief sketches within the larger story reveal the core of human darkness that Joseph Conrad identified as a source of destructive influence which, if ignored, as by Kurtz in *Heart of Darkness*, can destroy the individual and, at times, society. The mood of mystery and awe which surrounds such realities is Wolfe's own distinctive manner of handling the **theme** of darkness and reflects his ambiguous attitude to the South, where mob rule and social injustice are symptoms of a moral failure, but where a dream of honor and righteousness prevails. Gradually the dream of a golden city will draw George northward, but the South is the source of the organic life of his being.

Note

"The Hound of Darkness" - The title recalls Conrad's title, "Heart of Darkness," and the **theme** of that novel, but is also a variation on the title of the Victorian poet Francis Thompson's "The Hound of Heaven." In the poem, the sinner is pursued by a hound, who represents a personal God; here George Webber is tormented by an opposite force, an impersonal destructive impulse that is generated mysteriously in the dark chambers of human consciousness.

CHARACTER ANALYSES

Aunt Mag

A bitter narrow woman, a hypochondriac. It is she who caused George to be taken from his father. It is probably her enthusiasm as a Baptist for strict righteousness that alienated George from religion.

Uncle Mark

A bitter disillusioned man who sounds like Eugene's father, Oliver Gant, when he screams out against his wife. But unlike Oliver, who had no fear of human encounter or publicity, Mark takes his antagonisms into the hills where he joins the storm within him to the elements.

THE WEB AND THE ROCK

BOOK III: THE WEB AND THE WORLD

....

CHAPTERS 10-16

In 1916 George Webber's father dies, leaving him the inheritance which enables him to attend a small Baptist college, Pine Rock. There he meets and is looked after by Jim Randolph, a football hero who likes to brag that in his previous career as salesman he had possessed women in every state except Oregon-which he failed to visit. He also falls under the influence of Gerald Alsop, a Junior who gathers younger students about him and dispenses moral and aesthetic advice. But gradually George falls away from Alsop and toward the sins of the flesh. His crowning disgrace occurs when, after reading Dostoevski, he contends against the sentimental Alsop and his clique that the Russian is a better novelist than Dickens. The entire group screams in protest. It is at this time that George begins to write.

After college George goes to New York City and shares an apartment with four young men from Pine Rock, including Jim

Randolph, who has returned wounded from World War I. Jerry Alsop, too, has come to the city to establish a coterie but George again fights with him, this time about his own writing, and the relationship is permanently severed. The friendship between George and Jim is similarly deteriorating now that Jim is discovering that the past triumphs of the football field are not to be relived. After a bitter disagreement over his authority, all of the former Pine Rock students go separate ways. George, living alone and writing feverishly and formlessly, dreams of meeting a young widow and becoming her paramour and of the success and luxury that follows.

Comment

The college experience of George is a measure of the distance between Eugene Gant and this new hero. Eugene was the Genius, in conflict with the conventional. George is relatively typical-he goes on a college football weekend, feels admiration for the athlete, and gives in to normal gregarious impulses. Even his discovery of Dostoevski is on a lower key than Eugene's intellectual escapades which carry him through the whole range of Great Books. It is appropriate that he should be of middle height and have the ape-like torso of his father, because this confirms his place in the Darwinian; tradition; his origins and inherited tendencies are as ape-like as any other man's. His nickname, "Monk," testifies to his sharing in animality as it does to his participation in the quest of the bookish medieval monk for meaningful existence.

In his experiences in the city, too, George is a typical explorer. He can interest himself in the Dempsey-Firpo fight as a representation of the brutal, swift violence of American life.

And when he writes, he concentrates on an area of common experience, attempting, in "The End of the Golden Weather," to recapture the change which takes place in a boy's vision of the world between the ages of 12 and 13 when the golden dreams give way to a more troubled view-a change which took place in his own life and which he has seen validated in the city.

Life in the city contributes to George's alienation from the South. In college, he had become aware of the hypocrisy of the elder generation which preaches justice but refuses to let all men vote. But isolated in New York with his friends, he comes to see in them a failure of Southern leadership. Alsop is a pathetic figure in the city as he tries to surround himself with a sympathetic coterie, not wanting to give up his role as an arbiter of taste and moral values, but not wanting to be left out of new fads. Jim Randolph is a failure because he refuses to accept the responsibilities of adult life. George had looked to them as substitute fathers. But now, each of these Southern romantics, nurtured in provincial surroundings, believing in the strength of a personal magnetism, inherits an appropriate hell of loneliness and aimlessness. And George then must face the city on his own, with his dreams for companionship.

His dream of success takes the form of a chance encounter with a rich, 24-year-old widow. Having found and returned her lost purse, he eventually comes to enjoy her person and to dwell in her house, with its fabulous library, paying her 15 dollars a month rent in order to retain his self-respect, and soon winning success as a writer. This comically exaggerated dream might seem excessive if it were not that it so typifies the young man's yearning for fellowship and fame that it serves as a point of reference for George's future attainment.

Note

"Gotterdammerung" - "Twilight of the Gods," an appropriate title for the chapter on the destruction of the leadership of Jim Randolph. He is a modern Nordic god.

CHARACTER ANALYSES

Jim Randolph

A handsome athlete and military officer who, because of the immaturity of his view of life, is constantly searching for the lost glory of the football field. At the end all turn against him, even the girls he had so easily conquered. We learn that he is to die an early death.

Gerald Alsop

Fat and humorous, but with a viciousness disguised as levity. He is the Mother Machree of the campus, giving advice to younger students, especially about their personal life, always agreeing with conventional Southern attitudes. He is able to persuade himself and those around him that the president of the college and a local preacher are great men.

Randolph Ware

A literary researcher and teacher. George receives from him an assignment to write a novel; and this begins his pursuit of a literary career.

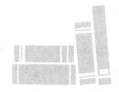

THE WEB AND THE ROCK

BOOK IV: THE MAGIC YEAR

. . . .

CHAPTERS 17-28

Book IV moves ahead to 1925. George is on a ship returning from Europe when he begins an affair with Esther Jack, a rich married woman. In New York, George fails to hear from Esther and so he sends her an angry letter. She arranges to meet him and they continue their affair while George is teaching in the School for Utility Cultures. Through Esther, who is a set designer, he comes into contact with the theatre, its operation and its habitues, as well as with the life of wealth.

There are tremors in this relationship. George begins to see signs of corruption in the world which Esther frequents. And an ugly anti-semitism begins to color his thinking about Esther's Jewish friends. But yet he recognizes her as an admirable craftsman, one who cannot stand shoddy work, and as a person of faith and integrity. Eventually Monk moves into a flat which Esther has rented for them to work in. She refuses to let him share the expenses, but any qualms about a loss of independence do not restrain him from returning her extravagant ecstasies and pledges of eternal love.

Comment

Esther is a stage in George's development. She replaces past figures of authority, male and female. She is Helen in her beauty and spirit. And like a father, she would teach him to work like a man. Also, she is a shortcut to knowledge. Traveled and cultivated, she knows many important persons in business, art, and literature. She knows about the city and about the maze of appearance and reality of the theatre. Because she is half-Jewish, she can introduce him to a culture of which he is timid and suspicious. Further, she has in her own life a web of experience that goes back in time and includes reminiscences of her father, an actor, and his friends, and their lost quests.

That this love affair is inadequate is obvious from a comparison of Esther and the lady of George's dream. Although this woman is wealthy, she is attached; she has a husband and a grown daughter. She is 20 years older than the imaginary widow. And she does pay the rent. Further, she is a successful set designer, basking in the limelight which George desires.

The ultimate breach will be a matter of destiny. George is a pilgrim and he must travel alone. One time, he visits Esther's theatre and discovers three ladies backstage sewing costumes. They suggest the three fates who weave the patterns of human existence, and anticipates the hapless doom which, for all their mutual joy, hangs over the lovers. The ship on which they first met represented their tentative relationship. George has made the temporary incursion into first class, but this is not his deck and ultimately he must return to steerage.

Note

"Penelope's Web" - The cloth which Ulysses' wife wove in order to put off her suitors. Here the parallel is suggested because of Esther's actual working with needle and cloth and because of the web of memories which she weaves into a meaningful fabric.

CHARACTER ANALYSIS

Esther Jack

Although youthful in appearance and quite beautiful in the opulent manner that Wolfe liked, she is, upon her meeting with George, 44 years old (Stephen Hook in *You Can't Go Home Again* p. 251, reckons her age at 48 in 1929). She is clever, resourceful, witty, and, although there is some hint of previous affairs with young men, faithful to George. The fact that she is married and has a grown daughter does not impede her reckless love.

THE WEB AND THE ROCK

BOOK V: LIFE AND LETTERS

. . . .

CHAPTERS 29-35

George continues to work on his story, "The End of the Golden Weather." Meanwhile, arguments about the theatre and bitter jealousy spring up between him and Esther. Attending a Greenwich Village party with Esther, his antagonism for her friends increases. Also, he begins to desire more freedom.

When he finishes his novel, acting on Esther's suggestion, he submits it to the publishers, Rawng and Wright. During the many weeks of waiting, tensions increase and many more quarrels occur. When George receives a letter of rejection, Esther then has him give the book to the writer, Seamus Malone, who passes it on to an agent. This revives George's spirits some, but when he meets Malone at a party, he finds the man to be an insufferable prig with nothing but contempt for contemporary writers.

Comment

One reason for the increased friction between Esther and George is professional jealousy, and this is further aggravated when George must depend on Esther for literary contacts. Another is in the nature of his quest. He is the pilgrim lost in the vastness of America, and so turns to a substitute mother for affection and a steadying hand, but he hates himself for needing such help and projects his hatred on the giver.

In keeping with his partly satiric intentions, Wolfe puts the climactic arguments into dramatic form. It is as if he is conscious of the falseness of the sentimental domestic tragedy, and so turns it into **burlesque**. But this comic technique does not detract from the seriousness of the **theme** of self-realization. George is beginning to manifest the same cruel violence that was seen earlier in the Libya Hill butcher, in Dick Prosser and the posse that captured him, and in his Uncle Mark. Here George's rancor and prejudice pour forth in a howling stream of invective that recalls the mad ranting of Uncle Mark. It is a black destructive force that will continue to mar his life until he can purge it.

Another **theme** which runs through the novel but which becomes strong here is the wasteland **theme** of death which is a result of a failure of communion. Wolfe constantly repeats variations on T.S. Eliot's phrase, "rats' alley/Where the dead men lost their bones." This suggests that Esther and George are in the condition of living death which characterizes the lovers in *The Waste Land*.

Another dark **theme** is the effect of time on human relationships. The joy of George and Esther has been limited by time: she is 20 years older than he. The song of time is a sad **refrain** which accompanies the passing of life: "And still the cat crept trembling at its merciless stride along the ridges of the backyard fence. The hoof and wheel went by upon the street. And high above the fabulous walls and towers of the city, the sound of time, murmurous and everlasting, brooded forever in the upper air." The iambic beat that runs through most of Wolfe's writing becomes more pronounced in such moments of poetic intensity. The paragraph might be arranged in a loose iambic **pentameter**, thus:

And still the cat crept trembling at its merciless stride along the ridges of the backyard fence. The hoof and wheel went by upon the street And high above the fabulous walls and towers of the city, the sound of time, murmurous and everlasting, brooded forever in the upper air.

Note

"The Ring and the Book" - Chapter 29. Browning's long poem of this title begins with a tribute to his wife. Here George, writing his book with great excitement, is enthusiastic in his praise sweetheart Esther. Possibly Wolfe is suggesting that this love affair, like the one depicted by Browning, is to culminate in a romantic tragedy.

THE WEB AND THE ROCK

BOOK VI: LOVE'S BITTER MYSTERY

. . . .

CHAPTERS 36-43

George feels that he is a failure. His arguments with Esther become more serious, until finally, in order to definitely end their relationship and prevent reconciliation, he books passage to Europe.

Comment

The title of the first chapter of this book, "A Vision of Death in April," suggests its pathetic mood. It is April-as in Eliot's *Waste Land*-but there is no new life in a land of the living dead. Both George and Esther evoke pity as they despair of success and love. At the same time, there is considerable comedy in this bleak section of the novel. For example, several pages are devoted to a mock-heroic treatment of George's "squeal" - the goat - like cry of joy which he seems to have lost. The sad farewell letter from Esther is interspersed with parentheses containing George's acid comments and descriptions of his furious gestures; the total effect is comic.

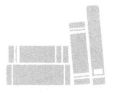

THE WEB AND THE ROCK

BOOK VII: OKTOBERFEST

....

CHAPTERS 44-50

In Europe, his love for Esther returns and he is filled with joy whenever he receives a letter from her, plunged into despair when he does not. He visits London, Paris, and Munich, absorbing the personality of each place. In Munich he attends the Oktoberfest, a beer celebration, and gets into a fight in which his face is smashed. He revives in a hospital with his face looking more like an ape's than ever. He now has the time to pause and examine his life. The last few pages are a dialogue between himself (or his Soul) and his Body. He seems to have acquired some freedom from his old hatreds and some measure of calm. In the last line of the novel, the Body tells him, "But-you can't go home again."

Comment

By the end of the novel, Webber has learned that he must participate in the rough give-and-take of life, that he is limited by his ape-inherited flesh, that he must sweat and labor like any craftsman. Esther has contributed her part in this development. She has taught him the value of sheer labor. Now he can advance to the next stage of maturity. Calmer, saner, more a "monk" - a detached man of letters - he can write an objective piece of literature. After the brutal violence of the Oktoberfest, the blackness inside him has been purged, and the education of the provincial has reached an important intermediary stage. He is ready to return to his own land with tolerance and understanding and the realization that he cannot recover the past. Wolfe stated that his projected third novel could be called "*'You Can't Go Home Again'*-which means back home to one's family, back home to one's childhood, back home to the father one has lost, back home to romantic love, to a young man's dreams of glory and of fame, back home to exile, to escape to 'Europe' and some foreign land, back home to lyricism, singing just for singing's sake, back home to aestheticism, to one's youthful ideas of the 'artist,' and the all-sufficiency of 'art and beauty and love,' back home to the ivory tower, back home to places in the country, the cottage in Bermuda away from all the strife and conflict of the world, back home to the father one is looking for-to someone who can help one, save one, ease the burden for one, back home to the old forms and systems of things that once seemed everlasting, but that are changing all the time-back home to the escapes of Time and Memory." (*Letters,* pp. 711-712). An axiom to this rule might be the fact that one must be ready for change and be able to respond to it in a detached manner-even when the change is the metamorphoses of human faces into swine-like snouts, as with his fellow drinkers in the beer hall.

YOU CAN'T GO HOME AGAIN

TEXTUAL ANALYSIS

BOOK I: THE NATIVE'S RETURN

....

CHAPTERS 1-9

Plot Analyses

Returning to New York City from Europe, George Webber attempts a more rational organization of his life. Though he resumes his affair with Esther Jack, he feels he is in control since they meet in his apartment and not, as before, in a shared one. The acceptance of his novel by James Rodney and Co. Publishers and the subsequent development of a close relationship with his editor, Foxhall Edwards, increases his confidence. There is a new objectivity in his manner as he observes the people around him, for example, his neighbor Mr. Katamoto, a Japanese sculptor who dies prematurely.

Chapters 6-9 describe George's return home for the funeral of Aunt Maw. On the Libya Hill pullman coach (K 19) he meets Nebraska Crane, a boyhood friend who has become a professional baseball player, as well as several of Libya Hill's prominent citizens who attempt to persuade Nebraska to invest in the town, and Judge Rumford Bland, a notorious sinner, blind from syphilis, who made his living by lending money to Negroes at exorbitant rates of interest. Bland, speaking with the authority of a blind prophet, asks George, "Do you think you can really go home again?" Then he predicts to the town leaders the impending doom of Libya Hill. Staying with an old friend, Randy Shepperton, George finds everywhere in the town a whirlwind of credit trading in land. Even Randy, a cash register salesman obligated to sell when there is no demand, is caught up in the inflationary spirit of the time.

Comment

It is important to distinguish between the author Thomas Wolfe and the fictional hero, George Webber, who is also a novelist. The former is a distinct but complex individual who reveals himself in this novel only under the guise of the omniscient author as he provides general comment on the significance of George's experiences. Although obviously a product of Wolfe's technique of holding a mirror up to himself, George Webber represents the writer as a modern Everyman-a much simpler and more universal character than the extremely autobiographical Eugene Gant.

Wolfe, now in his mid-thirties, has been making such personal discoveries as his need to evolve from a lyrical, ivory tower writer to an objective one, capable of seeing in and around people, molding characters who are amalgams rather than immediate copies of life, and able to articulate a more impersonal attitude to these characters. This accounts for the new style - the preponderance of direct, rather than indirect or dramatic, treatment of characters, the attempts at generalization, and the overt use of allegory.

George Webber represents a simpler version of this change as, viewing his recent experience, he realizes that he is like the rest of man in his limitations. He humbly and patiently explores the hearts of others, for instance, Mr. Katamoto, for whom George comes to feel respect and affection. Although some critics have questioned his relevance to the novel, Mr. Katamoto expresses in a preliminary way **themes** crucial to the development of George's sense of the world outside himself. Here is a highly developed "microscopic" aesthetic sensibility, a result of centuries of cultural refinement, prostituted in the American market for the production of grossly stupendous public monuments. At this time the full significance of the **episode** is muted, but it is a preparation for the exploration of reasons for the failure of an advanced civilization and the surge of brutality which George is to witness in Germany and, though in less detail, Japan. Here, too, is a representation of the ironic situation of man the maker, capable of producing permanent art objects but incapable of extending by one jot the brief span of his own life. George also reveals a new detachment in his personal relationships, for example, when he refuses to share in Esther's pledge of eternal love. There is a maturity in his ability to listen to the leaders of Libya Hill, whom he despises, and to attend the funeral of Aunt Maw without expressing any rancor. He can even stand the tongue of Delia Flood, who shares his funeral car and talks about real estate and, with gruesome detail, describes the exhumation of his mother's body. The native returns to America and then to his home town, but finds that both he and the place have changed so much as to prohibit any real going home. With a calm, dispassionate gaze, he reassesses the past. Obviously, *You Can't Go Home Again* is to be less a romantic justification of self than Wolfe's previous novels.

You Can't Go Home Again - The title expresses the main theme. Characters constantly try to go back to one or another kind of home and to recover the past. The use of the word home in such expressions as "The Home Coming" is ironic. Man cannot go back because he and the rest of the world are in constant state of flux. He must be ready to change, to grow, if he is to remain human.

CHARACTER ANALYSES

George Webber

An artistic Everyman, he represents that point of development where the writer finally begins to discover that he cannot go home, that he must grow. Although he might try to fool himself at first, he is discovering that freedom, detachment, and humility are necessary qualities. Since he is in a state of transition, many of his characteristics are balanced by opposing ones; for example, his egotism by his tender concern for others, his learnedness and the sophistication of his **allusions** by his anti-intellectualism.

Esther Jack

George's married mistress is in her late forties but beautiful. An extremely talented set designer, she is a shining light in a Park Avenue society that prizes money and easy culture. For George she is a mother-substitute as well as sweetheart and would provide him with protective warmth and tenderness. And since she is half-Jewish and possessed of many Jewish friends, she can challenge the provincial prejudices of George and help him to develop tolerance. But George is to discover that he can't go home again-even to this woman whom he loves.

Nebraska Crane

Part Cherokee. As a professional baseball player, he is as fearless and sanguine as when he was George's boyhood protector in Libya Hill. He is an unabashed exponent of the American Dream of returning to the simple life-he looks forward to the day when he can retire to a farm. He is one of the few characters in Wolfe's fiction who is to achieve his ambition.

Judge Rumford Bland: Blandly, he admits his own sins and predicts the outcome of the sins of others. Though this aging sinner has achieved a dignity born of honesty, he represents the inevitable decay of Southern family and tradition resulting from the exploitation of the Negro.

The Civic Leaders

"Parson" Flack, Baxter Kennedy, the Mayor, and Jarvis Riggs, the banker, are introduced here because they are the minds behind the false vision of prosperity that is to ruin Libya Hill.

Randy Shepperton

George's childhood Mercutio, knowledgeable about the world but not about the destruction of his own identity which his career as cash register salesman is leading to.

YOU CAN'T GO HOME AGAIN

BOOK II: THE WORLD THAT JACK BUILT

....

CHAPTERS 10-21

The omniscient author intrudes on the morning rituals of Esther Jack and her husband in their luxurious apartment on the day of a party which Esther had persuaded George to attend. Then time and scene are shifted: two elevator operators and a doorman below stairs prepare for work that evening. An antagonism develops between Henry, a union organizer, and old John, whose attitude to the tenants is one of docile servility. At the party, George, unnerved by all the glamor and sophistication, retreats into his shell and begins to look with jaundiced eye upon all around him. The phoniness and corruption disgust him and he decides that he must sever connections with Esther Jack and her world. The planned **climax** of the party, a miniature circus of wrought wire animals and performers created and conducted by Piggy Logan, increases George's animadversion. Meanwhile, a fire has broken out in the building and the guests are directed to the street, all escaping safely except the two elevator operators who are trapped and burned to death. The management, by arrangement with the police, silences news of the deaths.

Comment

Because of Wolfe's intention of increasing the distance between himself and his hero, and in keeping with George Webber's role as Everyman humbly struggling forward, the author allows the reader to infer many things which the **protagonist** is only beginning to realize as he carefully moves forward planting one foot before the other. The title "The World That Jack Built," contains a pun. Mr. Jack, the husband of Esther, infinitely more productive than the Jack of the child-song who only built a house, has built a world of dependents, culture, and riches around him. But let no one be misled. It is a world bought with a lot of jack-in the colloquial sense. The reader immediately recognizes in this seemingly deferential and unassuming man a symbol of the privilege, power, and indulgence that jack brings. This world is a false one. The Park Avenue building in which the Jacks live, built precariously over a train tunnel, is a symbol of the false security of that society. (At one point Mrs. Jack feels the "tremor" of the train below, then recalls a banker's remark concerning "Faint tremors in the market"). The disguised warfare between Mrs. Jack and her maids and between the doorman and the tenants is a symptom of social disorder. The party with its phony intellectuals, sham art, and pretentious conversation masks a moral bankruptcy.

The fire which routs the party is a symbol of the imminent social cataclysm of the Depression. Henry, the doorman, survives because he is the evolving working class, as tough and aggressive as those he serves-or, rather, refuses to serve-and willing to fight for his rights. It is possibly significant that the tenants are in his

BRIGHT NOTES STUDY GUIDE

hands at the end as he takes over the operation of the elevator. The stopping of the underground trains in order to safely flood the basement of the apartment house, an evidence of the power of privilege, also suggests the stopping of time which the social conflagration will produces.

Even George, lacking hindsight and omniscience and the power of rapid flight, can see that this world of Jack is false, that the "hollow pyramid of a false social structure had been erected and sustained upon a base of common mankind's blood and sweat and agony." He sees the inner corruption in this collection of callous pretenders and the threat to his honesty, and so frees himself from Esther Jack to look for "some nobler height," deciding that he must go with the "tide" that "was running in the hearts of men" -presumably the tide of social reform.

CHARACTER ANALYSES

Frederick Jack

Powerful in his financial dealings, pampered and protected in his domestic life. He is broad-minded enough to allow his wife to have a lover and even to bring the lover to his apartment for a party. He has complete confidence in his taste-which is bad-and in the rightness and permanence of the American economic empire of which he is a privileged member.

Nora Fogarty

Esther's unwashed and dipsomaniacal maid. Her war with Esther for moral superiority is a small version of the larger wars of social overthrow in the Thirties.

John Enborg

One of the victims of the fire is 64, hardworking, and militantly American. He is intolerant of those who do not work hard or who advocate social change.

Herbert Anderson

The other victim is a 25-year-old bachelor who teases old John about the girls.

Henry

"Organizin' Hank" is a serious and surly union advocate.

Lawrence Hirsch

A New York banker, elegant, smooth and capable of mouthing a few liberal expressions, but a ruthless financial tycoon and a corrupt and cruel pursuer of pretty women. He usually gets his way.

Piggy Logan

The creator and operator of a wire circus-all the rage with the smart set. Wolfe might have been witness to a similar entertainment provided by Alexander Calder, who created a circus of wire models which he operated for the entertainment of his friends before he invented his own art form of mobiles. If so, Wolfe reveals some intolerance in his portrayal of Piggy as a foolish eccentric.

YOU CAN'T GO HOME AGAIN

BOOK III: AN END AND A BEGINNING

CHAPTERS 22-26

The reaction to the publication of George's first novel creates new threats to his detachment. Irate letters from people in Libya Hill who recognize themselves in the book, flattery from the Lion Hunters, soul-tearing critical reviews are phenomena which the sensitive young writer finds difficult to handle. Gradually, however, he begins to adjust. He learns to look with contempt upon the Lion Hunters who attempt to use him. He learns to view praise or blame with equal caution. Meanwhile, the financial failure of Libya Hill lessens the town's concern with him. On March 12, 1930, a few months after the crash on Wall Street, the Citizen's Trust Company of Libya Hill collapses and Baxter Kennedy, the mayor, commits suicide. Randy, who has lost his job, pays a visit to George and, finding him in a state of transiency, criticizes him for playing the spoiled aesthete - the "wounded faun" - whom society misunderstands and persecutes. He advises him to move to a new apartment and make a fresh start.

Comment

The stock market crash and the publication of his novel in the fall of 1929 motivate George toward objectivity. After an uproar is created in Libya Hill by his book, he realizes he must try to understand the wounded South with its mixed heritage of slavery, deceit, and false pride which made it react so violently. Further, he discovers a kernel of valuable truth in the advice of the town drunk: "Why, hell! If George wants to write about a horse thief, that's all right. Only the next time I hope he don't give his street address. And there ain't no use in throwing in his telephone number, too." He realizes he must write with greater selectivity and invention. Another lesson in detachment is provided by the Lion Hunters who, as George learns to his sorrow, are only interested in exploiting him.

The financial **catastrophe**, especially when it reaches Libya Hill, also has a tempering effect. George can see in his home town a representation of the whole force of the depression, which results not merely from the breakdown of the capitalist system but because of "the ruin of the human conscience" in the men who saw "the emptiness and hollowness of their lives." The suicide of jovial Baxter Kennedy in the privy in Judge Bland's building is a perfect stroke. It is as if he would go home to his father, to the office which Kennedy's and Bland's fathers once shared, their names still dimly visible on the window shades; as if, in this final gesture of abasement, to recognize his brotherhood in corruption with the usurer, Bland, and the accuracy of his prophecy of "impending ruin."

With the aid of Randy, he realizes that there is some falseness in his first book in his posture as the tormented artist. He sees too that he must work for a firmer structure and more universal **themes** - the kind of larger vision which

Wolfe achieves successfully for the first time in *You Can't Go Home Again*. Ironically, Randy, who brings George to these mature considerations, is himself doomed because of blindness about himself. Absolutely confident in his credentials as a supersalesman, he goes about searching for a new job, but finds nothing and is forced to go on relief. Later, we learn that he soon dies. The parallel with the career of Romeo's ironic and self-confident friend, Mercutio, is sustained.

Notes: *Home To Our Mountains*-George's first novel, published at the time of *Look Homeward, Angel,* is autobiographical, and obviously extremely close to Wolfe's actual first novel. Some caution should be observed however in applying George's discussion of this novel to the feelings Wolfe had about *Look Homeward, Angel*. George's experiences are an exaggeration of Wolfe's.

Man-Creating and Man-Alive-Used in George's letters to Randy to distinguish between his role as author, which is impersonal, and his life as a man of conscience, sensitive to the feelings of others, now torn with guilt because of his recognition that he has betrayed the people of Libya Hill.

YOU CAN'T GO HOME AGAIN

BOOK IV: THE QUEST OF THE FAIR MEDUSA

· ·

CHAPTER 27-31

George has taken Randy's advice and moved into a basement apartment in south Brooklyn where he works furiously on a new novel. A marked increase in charity colors his relations with other people, his neighbors, Mr. Marple, a lonely widower who works for an insurance company, and Mr. Wakefield, a dotty old Civil War veteran, and the lonely, homeless men who sleep the night in subway stations. At the same time, George is constantly disciplining himself to observe reality carefully and to capture it in minute detail.

In Chapter 28 the scene shifts to the apartment of his editor, Foxhall Edwards. In warm terms, the simplicity, honesty and restraint of "The Fox" are depicted. His insight-his ability to read the news behind the news-is illustrated in Chapter 29 where a newspaper article describing a suicide prompts an imaginative construction of the personal and social circumstances of such an event. Chapter 30 is a pessimistic, personal analysis of the inhumanity which reigns in America and throughout the world. Chapter 31, "The Promise of America," beautifully sings the praise of the grandeur of America and its magnificent promise for its future leaders - the seekers.

Comment

The move to south Brooklyn is a resumption of George's pilgrimage. The path to the golden city leads through the jungle life of the slums. He attempts to be involved in the life outside himself, to see it clearly and wholly. By the synthesizing power of the imagination, with an involvement of head and heart, he would bring together all of life. His nearness to the Gowanus Canal and his excursions to the subways and privies where the disenfranchised of the earth huddle together represent his contact with the depths. His frequent walks on Brooklyn Bridge are prompted by his aspiration to commune with far-flung islands of experience in order to evolve a coherent view of life. His description of the ages of man (pp. 432-436) is a product of his desire for understanding.

The arduousness of his task is revealed in the title of this book "The Quest of the Fair Medusa." He is like Perseus who, faced with the task of conquering Medusa whose gaze turned men to stone, discovered a formula for making himself invisible and then cut off her head. George feels he must achieve the fame represented in the Fair Medusa - but he must first learn to make himself invisible in order to escape calcification. To do this means to avoid a too personal or subjective - a "wounded faun" - approach to his art. It also means to escape from the rigidity which fame can cause when the lionized writer sells himself to society and refuses to take the risk of altering his previous style.

Wolfe might have recalled Shelley's description of Medusa's tormented face:

"'Tis the melodious hue of beauty thrown Athwart the darkness and the glare of pain, Which humanize and harmonize the strain."

A difficult mistress, to win her the writer has to fathom the darkness and the glare of pain-which George is to do in subsequent chapters, until he is capable or realizing, after encountering Fame's minion, Lloyd McHarg, that even his present concept of fame is a limited and dangerously confining one. But for now, the Medusa is his challenge.

The portrayal of "Fox" Edwards is sympathetic, but perhaps even here Wolfe is suggesting the reason for George's subsequent break with his friend (paralleling Wolfe's own rift with Maxwell Perkins). Fox is sympathetic to his fellow men but, because he believes in the inevitability of human failure, does nothing to help. His attitude resembles the impersonality of T. S. Eliot. In contrast to his moral restraint and reluctance to actively work to change the world, George's own trend is away from the self and toward his neighbor. Wolfe might be attempting to suggest the limitations of Fox by frequently using in this section materials from Eliot's poetry. For example, in the first paragraph of Chapter 27 lonely men are leaning on window sills as in "Prufrock," and in Chapter 29, "The Hollow Men," Wolfe varies Eliot's **theme** of society's moral hollowness by defending the man who commits suicide as the one man capable of independent action-even if he is literally a hollow man, his blood having splashed out, appropriately, on his fellow man. This Chapter 29 is also a development of Wolfe's technique of comparing the magnificent past, here represented by Sir Francis Drake, with the limited present in which the only adventurer is the suicide victim. It is as if Wolfe is getting out of his system the techniques of 1920s writing in order to move into the new decade with the maturity and control with which to forge a message in harmony with the tide that is running in the hearts of men.

If George is learning about loneliness, he is also increasing his love of life - this is the significance of "The Promise of America." Wolfe's giantism is brilliantly revealed in his descriptions of the individual's desire to absorb the plenty of the land. He beckons the seeker - the universal spirit of youth and discovery -to reach from his vantage point on the Rocky Mountains and "dip a hatful of cold water on Lake Michigan," to take his shoes off and "work your toes down in the river oozes of the Mississippi bottom." The promise of America demands an active quest for life.

Notes: Locusts - Symbolic of the swarm of life which Wolfe must learn to control.

Anodyne-In Chapter 30, no anodyne-drug to alleviate pain-can be found for America.

CHARACTER ANALYSES

Foxhall Edwards

A restrained New Englander educated at Groton and Harvard, he has taste and a sense of humor, deplores injustice, hatred, and the exploitation of man by man, but is essentially a conservative. As George's editor, he became his closest friend and spiritual father, but, as if to express the distance that separates the editor from the writer, Wolfe includes no scenes where George and Fox are together.

C. Green

An unidentified man, 35 years old, who committed suicide by jumping from the twelfth floor of the Admiral Francis Drake Hotel.

YOU CAN'T GO HOME AGAIN

BOOK V: EXILE AND DISCOVERY

. . . .

CHAPTERS 32-37

Book V finds George in London, competently looked after by his English cook and cleaning lady, Daisy Purvis. Here he meets the prominent American writer, Lloyd "Knuckles" McHarg, who has given public praise to George's first novel. McHarg, on a European tour, stops off in London and invites George to call on him. Then he takes George on a trip to a friend's house in Surrey. He insists, too, that George accompany him on a tour of Britain, a prospect which is horrifying to George. Fortunately, after the much interrupted trip to Surrey, during which McHarg collapses several times due to drink and fatigue, nothing more is said about the tour.

Comment

With the pilgrimage to England George's view of life continues to expand. If Daisy Purvis is a delight to have around the house, she nevertheless represents a political obtuseness which accepts the inevitability of poverty and privilege and which fosters the worship of the English Royal Family. The experience with Lloyd McHarg is almost a direct record of Wolfe's own meeting with Sinclair Lewis, and Wolfe has been accused of betraying a friendship. But Lewis himself, with some humor, merely objected to Wolfe's exaggerated emphasis on his drinking and the size of his knuckles. But however dangerously close to reality, the **episode** does have its value in terms of the symbolic structure of the novel. For McHarg is the Fame which George has been seeking. And he hears from the lips of the older writer the counsel to beware of freezing up as a result of fame, and he sees in McHarg's frustration and exhaustion the limits of fame. There is a paralysis of faculties-dramatically represented here-which comes from another sort of intimacy with fame than that previously dreaded by George. Here is the man who, after conquering fame, has nothing further to work for, and so stumbles, a victim of the Fair Medusa. George assesses this new pitfall.

This **episode** is also an opportunity for George to make some observations. The proposed trip through England is McHarg's idea for capturing the past. Perhaps it is a realization that you can't go home again that causes him to drop the suggestion. The actual overnight trip to Surrey is a retreat away from the city with its complex problems of life. McHarg's friend, Reade, has fled from the city to the protections of country life. This author of slight critical biographies represents for George a tribe of futilitarians, like the rural aesthetes of America, who run away from the competition of the city to an affectedly artistic semi-existence in the country. In a sense, Daisy, McHarg, and Reade are all trying to recover the past, to go home again to a less complex way of life, and in doing so they tend to freeze into the posture of caricature.

Notes: The Little People-Britain's poor, who become visible to George as a breed set apart, a result of generations of deprivation.

Babbitt-Sinclair Lewis's novel about a typical businessman, George Babbitt, whose name has come to be synonymous with self-interest and Rotarian hypocrisy.

CHARACTER ANALYSES

Daisy Purvis

Loyal to country and employer, she represents the prideful diligence of the English worker. But there is an inhumanity to her as well as a crippling egoism.

Lloyd "Knuckles" McHarg

Red-headed, reddish skinned, wiry, he combines an intensity of manner with a physical frailty that is constantly prostrating him. He is another spiritual father for George, kindly and wise, but perhaps overly possessive.

Ricenbach Reade

A good man but a failure in life because he refused to fight the battles of the city where the competition and criticism were strong and has retreated into the isolation of the country. His refusal to get involved in life is obvious in his refusal to have anything to do with McHarg until George assures him that he is not "sick."

George Webber

Begins to analyze life in a new way as he realizes that the true races of man are not defined by national frontiers or by definitions of anthropologists-but by occupations.

YOU CAN'T GO HOME AGAIN

. . . .

CHAPTERS 38-44

In the **climax** of the novel, in 1936, after a brief return to New York, George revisits Germany, the country for whose traditions he feels the greatest spiritual affinity. He is filled with joy at the acclaim given his writing by the Germans. He is happy with his German friends and with his mistress, Else von Kohler. But, becoming aware of the oppressions and secrecies of fascism, he decides to leave. On the day of his departure, his friend Heilig tells him that the reason he is read in Germany is because he is not overtly opposed to the Nazi Party and he begs George not to include any anti-Nazi material in future books. But this George refuses to promise.

At the station there is suspicion and bickering among three of George's friends, and later on the train the same mood of hostility prevails. It is not until George discovers that one of the others in his compartment is an American and a friend of

THE WEB AND THE ROCK AND YOU CAN'T GO HOME AGAIN

Foxhall Edwards that a conversation begins and then it is a while before the others join in. But at the Belgian border, all sense of comradeship is shattered when one of the five members of the compartment, a Jew trying to escape with his money, is arrested by German officials.

Comment

The **episode** on the train is an illustration of the kind of political writing which George is to do. It is a deliberate allegory calling for human understanding between the members of "The Family of the Earth." The train is a microcosm of world civilization as it moves forward in historical time. The Jew represents his race as it is being persecuted in Germany. The arresting officer, with his coarseness of manner, shaven head, and Kaiser Wilhelm moustache, is a representation of the brutality of the police state. And George, holding 10 marks of the man's money, feels his complicity in the brutal arrest about which he can do nothing; possibly too he feels guilt at his own prior anti-Semitism. For the four passengers who witness the arrest, the event represents a loss of "humanity;" for George especially it represents the loss of the highest sort of humanity, the civilization that was the goal of his quest.

George's disillusionment with Germany is tardy but decisive. Like the hero of the picaresque novel who wanders from place to place learning through observing, so George has traveled about acquiring an education in the school of life. Lionized as never before, he is not so starry-eyed as to fail to recognize Hitlerism for what it is. He is even capable of seeing in his friends elements of Germany's malady. For example the racism of Heilig who, although his own origins are under investigation, despises the Jews. After the **episode** on the train, George compares himself with Faust who has lost his Helen and all of the beauty and wisdom associated with Germany's traditions. He has discovered, then, another spiritual home to which he cannot return.

"The Dark Messiah" - Hitler, whom Wolfe sees as a cultural antichrist.

CHARACTER ANALYSES

Else Von Kohler

George's German mistress, a "perfect type of the Norse Valkyrie" - tall, with braided yellow hair, fair complexion. She is intelligent and prideful.

Franz Heilig

Librarian and linguistic scholar. Although seemingly detached in his approach to life, he has a lively fondness for George. He is George's closest male friend in Germany.

Karl Lewald

George's German publisher, a jolly and effervescent Babbitt.

YOU CAN'T GO HOME AGAIN

BOOK VII: A WIND IS RISING, AND THE RIVERS FLOW

· ·

CHAPTERS 45-48

George writes a long letter to Foxhall Edwards, reflecting on the experiences depicted in the novel. He has decided to break with fox. What he has seen of the world has convinced him that the great evil is greed and that Hitlerism is a modern manifestation of the ancient rapacity of the Barbarians, and that Fox's posture of noninvolvement is the wrong one. George intends now to make his writing the agency of his protest and so he announces his intention to find a new publisher. Love and Fame-his guiding angles till now have not been enough. His end now shall be to illuminate the tragic waste of America and of the world.

Comment

The progress of growth has come full cycle. George now feels he has become a socio-political writer interested not in his own lyrical impulses so much as in the welfare of mankind. This discovery is to provide structure and **theme** for a future novel- and if we change the name of George Webber to Thomas Wolfe, this is that novel.

But even in his enunciation of purpose, Webber changes. He realizes that this scope must be enlarged beyond contemporary Germany or America to include all-time and all-place; the prevalence of dog-eat-dog is not confined to one locale but is universal. The letter to Fox is not a mere summing up but rather an attempt to provide a last analysis of the present state of mind of the artist. The title of the first chapter in Book VII, "Young Icarus," suggests a new beginning, new experiments, and new flights on one's own wings, and, accordingly, in these last pages several new facets of Webber's mind are revealed: his ability to distinguish himself from the "lost generation" of the 20s; his power to synthesize all previous experience in terms of the "you can't go home again" **theme**; and his new objectivity of approach as, using the direct method, he speaks with a mature and dispassionate voice. This last book is not a mere resume. It is the test of all the growth that has taken place in "Monk" Webber - this Everyman who blends a primitive mountain toughness with a poetic pastoral yearning. His ape-like body suggests the aeons of evolution that he has undergone until finally he contemplates himself and says, look, this beast can think, and love, and fight with a pen. He recognizes that Fox might be right in his pose of fateful acceptance which emulates the attitude of the author of Ecclesiastes; he is the rock, built to endure all the chaos of city life. But George is the web, a plant of Southern growth, organic in his processes, defiant of all static principles including the principle of contradiction. So, although he may perceive that "Man was born to live, to suffer, and to die, and what befalls him is a tragic lot," he shouts defiance at this insipid truth: "But we must, dear Fox, deny it all along the way."

....

George Webber

Nicknamed "Monk," he has the physical appearance of an ape. Wolfe describes him in evening dress at the party at Jack's: "The low brow with its frame of short black hair, to the knees, and the curved paws gave him an appearance more simian than usual, and the image was accentuated by his not-too-well-fitting dinner jacket." His grotesque body violates the serene atmosphere of the party. But it is a token of his oneness with his fellow men who are also descendants-although less obviously-from the ape. It is a realization of this oneness with all men that contributes to George's sense of peaceful acceptance in this novel. Looking at his fellows with realistic eyes, he is able to learn the value of personal detachment and social attachment. He withdraws from the arena of personal contention and flings himself instead into the social revolution of the Thirties.

As an artistic Everyman, George travels from city to city, from country to country, seeking to discover himself and the world of the artist. His central quest in the baffling labyrinth of modern life is to find a language that is rich and varied as his artistic purposes. His journeys often take on the appearance of a return to a past home; but this is only illusory. His path inevitably leads outward to new homes, to new forms of expression.

By the end of the novel George has learned that he cannot go home again - not to any of the escapes into prior forms of existence that the imagination deludes man with. He has learned that Man-Creating (the representative artist) and Man-Alive (the artist as human being, with a conscience and natural connections with other men) should be one, that the artist puts the ideal of his conscience into his writing instead of making a sharp distinction between the Good and the Beautiful as George did in his first novel. And, about the world outside himself, he has learned that its most universal characteristic is change: there is no fixity, all is flux.

But the changes that occur in George in the course of the novel are not merely educational. Although he is a relatively simple character when compared with such a complex individual as Eugene Gant, he nevertheless is a developing personality. In a world of change, he too changes-decisively. His growth is in the direction of greater humility, freedom, artistic discipline, and humanity. The ending of the novel is hopeful because George is able to put a name on the evil that has plagued human history; it is greed, "single selfishness and compulsive greed." And he is able to commit himself to the battle against this evil and to accept the call "to leave the friends you loved, for greater loving." That is, he is ready to accept his monkish vocation, to become a part of the aspirations of all men. His total orientation of aesthetics, morality, and philosophy have changed in this world of flux.

Esther Jack

George's married mistress is 48 years old in 1929, when the novel opens, but she is beautiful. And she possesses a mixture of sensuality and humor that is so youthful that the reader is taken aback by occasional references to her age or by the appearance of her grown daughter, Alma. To Stephen Hook, her longtime friend, she is a representation of timelessness set against a world of decay. To George, she is this, and many other things as well. She is a mother-substitute who offers him protection and warmth, but who makes him despise himself for requiring such fortification. First appearing to Eugene Gant at the end of *Of Time and the River,* then encountering and aiding the apprentice writer, George Webber, in *The Web and the Rock,* finally serving as a challenge to George's independence in *You Can't Go Home Again,* she symbolizes the beauty and munificence which inspire, direct, and give substance to the idealistic dreams of the young writer; and she is retained as a symbol in the novels as long as she is capable of sustaining such illusions.

There is a practical side, too, to the relationship of George and Esther. He gives to her the love of a young man and sensual pleasures, as well as a youth for her to fondle. He gives to her an emotional satisfaction which her secure, smooth businessman of a husband cannot. He and she share aesthetic passions which defy the comprehension of the earthbound Mr. Jack. She gives to George many practical advantages. A talented set designer, she introduces George to the New York theatre, to the web of artistic cooperation which is to have some influence on his own career. Because she is half-Jewish, she represents a challenge to those provincialisms which George must overcome in himself if he is to become a writer of large vision. She provides financial as well as moral support for the aspiring writer. And her contacts with writers, literary agents and publishers make her contacts with writers, literary agents and publishers make her a valuable adviser. Part of the reason why she is removed from George's life when she is (after the party at her apartment), is because she has served her practical function. George's first novel has been accepted, and he now has established his own contacts. Her association merely represents a threat to his future artistic commitments. Her tolerance - once an important influence on George's educational development - now works to separate them, because she is tolerant of those persons, like the banker Lawrence Hirsch, who have come to represent for the young writer the principal evils in American society. Her ability to suspend time becomes a lie to George as he realizes that all life is flux.

Nebraska Crane

Not a central figure in terms of his contribution to plot but extremely important to the **theme** of George's self-discovery. In one incident in *The Web and the Rock,* he serves as a baseball player ex machina. George is about to be abused by a group of bullies when Nebraska fortunately arrives carrying a baseball bat. When one of the boys refuses to give ground, Nebraska socks him in the head with the bat. With no compunction, he tells George, after the bullies have retreated, that he would not have minded killing the boy. He represents a simple righteousness that would uphold a norm of boyhood justice at any cost, let the chips-or heads-fall where they may. He is as strong and fearsome as his Cherokee ancestors, or his father, a policeman and professional wrestler. More importantly for his influence on George, he is a stoic, accepting pain and hardship in the pursuit of duty. He is now a professional baseball player, a veteran of many years in the majors; his dream is to retire to a farm, after a few more years of play, there to live a life of simple productivity with his unaffected wife, Myrtle. When George meets him on the train to Libya Hill, he finds him to be as strong and fatalistic as ever. He easily withstands the efforts of the Libya Hill businessmen to induce him to invest in the town. He represents the rugged stoical vision which George is beginning to achieve as he manages to check his tendencies toward softness and romanticism.

Judge Rumford Bland

His importance in the novel, like Nebraska Crane's, is symbolic. His father was a prominent citizen in Libya Hill, a lawyer. He, too, was a practicing lawyer and, for a time, a judge. But he is now a ruined old man. He gave up law to practice usury, loaning money to Negroes at exorbitant rates of interest. Indeed, he has become something of a junkman, accepting the household articles of the Negroes as collateral for loans. He has been notorious as a whoremaster, and now his eyes are blinded with syphilis, his face is sunken, his body wasted with disease and age. He represents in his deterioration the failure of the South, which has been contaminated by slavery. When George sees him on the train to Libya Hill, his childhood fears of this ominous figure revive. And he is terrified when the old blind man somehow recognizes him and accosts him. The blind man speaks wisely, however, and predicts to George that he will not be able to go home again. To the others in the train, also, Bland is an object of terror. He predicts to the Libya Hil businessmen that the town is doomed. He indicts them as the cause. Mayor Kennedy, one of the passengers on the train, later makes a grotesque recognition of Bland's wisdom when, after the failure of the Citizen's Trust Company of Libya Hill, he commits suicide in the privy of Bland's building.

Randy Shepperton

George's best friend in Libya Hill is a bachelor who lives with his sister Margaret. He was George's childhood Mercutio, intelligent and quick and nobody's fool. George stays with him when he visits Libya Hill and finds his friend to have aged and weakened. The causes of his deterioration are in his job as a cash register salesman. When George visits Randy, he finds that the guest room has been given to Dave Merrit, an executive in Randy's firm who travels about spreading public good will. George happens to overhear a conversation between Merrit and Randy in which the executive is threatening the salesman, vehemently insisting that he increase his sales. George is embarrassed for his friend. As time goes on, Randy's identity becomes blurred. When he loses his job in the depression, his confidence in his ability as a supersalesman begins to wane. He is forced to throw himself upon the charity of relatives and eventually to go on relief. He dies during the depression.

Beside being a representation of the failure of the American free enterprise system, Randy contributes to the discoveries which George makes about himself. Because he is kind, tolerant, and perceptive, he is one of the few people in Libya Hill capable of making a balanced judgment of George's first novel. He comes to New York to visit George, correctly appraises his present position, advises him to move into a new apartment to begin a new life, and offers the sensible criticism that the first novel, although excellent, tended to portray the hero as too much the wounded fawn, the genius who is tormented by the insensitive multitude. He is a friend to whom George can write and speak with honesty, and he therefore provides the function of keeping George sane.

Foxhall Edwards

An extremely dedicated editor for Rodney Publishers, he adopts George and gives him guidance. Although Wolfe, for personal reasons, **refrains** from depicting George and Fox together in any scenes in the novel, he is clearly a friend, brother, and father-substitute for the young writer. Possibly, as with Esther, George despises himself for relying so heavily upon his editor.

At the conclusion of the novel, a long letter explains why George is breaking off his business relationship with his editor's firm. The letter bears a resemblance to a series of letters sent to Maxwell Perkins by Wolfe, announcing his decision to break with Scribners Publishers. George is going through the same crisis as Wolfe, although his explanation is perhaps a bit less complicated than Wolfe's. George points out that Fox is like the author of Ecclesiastes, a rock-like witness to the inevitability of evil's triumph. Although he hates injustice, he is resigned to it, and therefore will not fight to reform the world. George, on the other hand, feels compelled to commit himself to the cause of social justice. And so he leaves his friend to join with the "tide" that is running in the hearts of men.

The depiction of Fox is respectful and affectionate. His odd mannerisms, his interest in people, his fondness for his family, his dedication to literature are attractively described. But, nevertheless, he is a figure of stone and represents the status of conservative thought-while George's commitment must ultimately be to a world of change and flux.

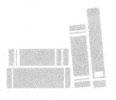

CRITICAL COMMENTARY

. . . .

PERSPECTIVES

Critical reaction to Wolfe has been diverse. There are those who have attended to the Wolfe "legend." They have viewed him as a giant of the imagination who poured out thousands of words without let up, whose primary gift was inspiration. There are those who because of formalistic bias have refused to recognize Wolfe as a significant author; for these he lacked the essential faculty of critical intelligence. Bernard De Voto's early indictment of Wolfe in the *Saturday Review of Literature* (April 25, 1936) as an immature writer lacking the ability to organize a novel has been repeated by numerous critics, even by some who are in the main sympathetic to his fiction. Such criticism generally fails to take into account the great flexibility of the novel form. Wolfe, like several other major writers of fiction-including Voltaire, Sterne, Goethe-sacrificed the conventional dramatic unity of the "well made" novel in order to create a more powerful vehicle of ideas and ideals.

Some students of Wolfe content themselves with tracking down the sources of his autobiographical novels. Such research is only valuable as an aid to the study of literature when it deals with the question of how Wolfe transformed the material taken from life. Many of the reminiscences devoted to Wolfe deal merely with the question of what were the facts concerning the life of Wolfe. Such a work as Floyd Watkins' *Thomas Wolfe's Characters: Portraits from Life* is much more valuable than other such biographical studies because it concerns itself with the author's special use of the materials of experience.

Others analyze Wolfe for his philosophy or social theory-finding him to be a vitalist, a democrat, an egalitarian, a primitive, a middle-class radical, a Marxist, a rightist, a confused socialist, an enlightened socialist, a Manichaean, a Victorian, a Puritan, a Romantic, a platonist, a neo-platonist, a naturalist, a lyricist or an American pioneer. All such attempts to treat Wolfe from a single point of view are falsifications of Wolfe's impulses. His work contains so many different strains of thought that he can be quoted as supporting almost any theory or political position. The trouble with such theory hunting is that it approaches Wolfe in a sectarian way, with bias, and fails to do justice to the diversity of his varied fabric.

Since his death in 1938 Wolfe's reputation has continued to grow and to take definite form. Popularly, he is conceived to be a great writer, a spokesman for the aspirations of identity-questing youth. He raises questions and hints at answers that evoke in many readers a sense of communion - "That was what I was thinking, that was what I was trying to say!" In presenting the history of the provincial's discovery of the world, he appeals to all who are or have been provincials, and he will continue to enjoy popularity as long as there are provincials in the world. His critical and scholarly reputation has focused on his articulation of the American experience, the quest of the individual living in an improvisatory culture, trying to create a world of social values to replace the disordered landscape of the past. He is the pioneer with a pen.

Although critics have tended to concentrate on *Look Homeward, Angel* as the most significant of Wolfe's novels, *You Can't Go Home Again,* probably his second most successful work, has also received considerable attention. But many critics are perplexed by this last novel. Herbert Muller, although he appreciates the relation of *You Can't Go Home Again* to the earlier novels as the fourth segment in a multi-novel creating the American myth, objects to such a failure of artistic concentration as is revealed in the lengthy recapitulatory letter to Foxhall Edwards at the end of the novel. C. Hugh Holman in his pamphlet on Wolfe sees *You Can't Go Home Again* as "much less a novel than *The Web and the Rock.*" Indeed, "The book - it is hardly a novel at all - has the very loose narrative structure of George Webber's life" (pp. 22-23). Bruce McElderry, Jr., in his recent book on Wolfe in the Twayne's United States Authors Series, objects to the substitution of generalized **exposition** for effective dramatic presentation in the last two novels. He also complains that the last novel is too episodic to achieve effective concentration; that the brief **episodes** with Nebraska Crane, Judge Bland, Mr. Katamoto, C. Green, and Daisy Purvis scatter rather than focus the attention. On the other hand, most critics have pointed out that the unity of idea is strongest in *You Can't Go Home Again.* All of the **episodes** illuminate the same **theme** - that one cannot return to whatever home the imagination constructs. Muller points out that the novel is also unified by the prevalence of representations of change-of flux as opposed to fixity. Pamela Hansford Johnson argues that the concluding letter to Foxhall Edwards is the natural culmination of tendencies in the novel. In spite of the fact that critics point out specific failings in the last two novels, there is a general consensus that *The Web and the Rock* and, especially *You Can't Go Home Again,* because they reveal a new side to Wolfe's talent as well as new ideas, add to his stature as a novelist.

Wolfe scholarship and criticism will never acquire the weight or complexity of commentary of that of modernist writers like Joyce-Wolfe is simply not that difficult. He does not need or easily yield to the techniques of detailed explication. However, the trends of future criticism might be anticipated. C. Hugh Holman in his pamphlet on Wolfe discusses Wolfe's view of man which is, like Whitman's, essentially romantic: "His total work stands, like so many monuments of romantic art, a group of fragments imperfectly bodying forth a seemingly ineffable cosmic vision in terms of the self of the artist" (p. 29). It is Wolfe's romantic vision of the individual as creature of infinite longings but of severe limitations of ability that might well be explored in future works on Wolfe. Too, the artistry of Wolfe in such an unconventional performance as *You Can't Go Home Again* might fruitfully be explored. His use of **imagery** of metamorphosis - the alteration of living flesh to stone, the use of a language of change, the shifting levels of consciousness as the mind penetrates from appearances to reality which in turn becomes appearance to a deeper level of reality - these contribute to the special quality of the novel in such a way as to invite critical analysis.

BIBLIOGRAPHY

Holman, C. Hugh, "Thomas Wolfe: A Bibliographical Study," *Texas Studies in Literature and Language,* I (Autumn, 1959), 427-445. Groups and appraises studies on Wolfe.

Johnson, Elmer D., *Of Time and Thomas Wolfe: A Bibliography with a Character Index of His Works*, New York: Scarecrow Press, 1959.

McElderry, Bruce R., Jr., *Thomas Wolfe,* New York: Twayne Publishers, 1964. Contains an annotated selected bibliography.

For articles and books published in recent years but not included in McElderry's bibliography, see the annual bibliography in *PMLA*.

Biography

Adams, Agatha Boyd, *Thomas Wolfe: Carolina Student,* Chapel Hill: University of North Carolina Library, 1950. Wolfe as a college student.

Nowell, Elizabeth, *Thomas Wolfe: A Biography,* Garden City: Doubleday, 1960. The authoritative biography. Detailed and comprehensive although it misleadingly offers many long quotations from Wolfe's novels as representations of actual experience. It also suffers somewhat from Miss Nowell's reluctance to discuss critically those associates whom she shared with Wolfe.

Watkins, Floyd C., *Thomas Wolfe's Characters: Portraits from Life,* Norman: University of Oklahoma Press, 1957. Combines history, biography, and criticism. Watkins discovers that a high percentage of characters, settings, and events in Wolfe's writing is based on actuality. He also points out the processes of transformation by which Wolfe turns the raw materials into fiction.

Criticism

Albrecht, W. P., "Time as Unity in Thomas Wolfe," *New Mexico Quarterly Review,* XIX (Autumn, 1949), 320-329. Included in *Walser, The Enigma of Thomas Wolfe.* Time provides the unifying **theme** in the novels.

Angoff, Charles, "Thomas Wolfe and the Opulent Manner," *Southwest Review,* XLVIII, vi-vii (1963), 81-84.

Baker, Carlos, "Thomas Wolfe's Apprenticeship," *Delphian Quarterly,* XXIII (January, 1940), 20-25.

Bishop, John Peale, "The Sorrows of Thomas Wolfe," *Kenyon Review,* I (Winter, 1939), 7-17. Sees Wolfe as resembling Hart Crane in his representation of the quality of American life. Wolfe's failure to achieve a total structure is a result of his inability to control the shifting reality of America.

Brown, E. K., "Thomas Wolfe: Realist and Symbolist," *University of Toronto Quarterly,* X (Jan., 1941), 153-166. Also in *Enigma.* Sees Wolfe's symbolism as counterbalancing his **realism** and "roomy autobiography," and claims that if Wolfe had live he would have continued the clarification of his symbols.

Budd, Louis J., "The Grotesques of Anderson and Wolfe," *Modern Fiction Studies,* V (Winter, 1959-1960), 304-310.

Carpenter Frederic I., "Thomas Wolfe: The autobiography of an Idea," *University of Kansas City Review,* XII (Spring, 1946), 179-187.

Church, Margaret, "Thomas Wolfe: Dark Time," *Publications of the Modern Language Association,* LXIV (September, 1949), 629-638. Also in *Enigma.*

Cowley, Malcolm, "Thomas Wolfe," *Atlantic Monthly,* CC (Nov., 1957), 202-212.

Delakas, Daniel L., "Thomas Wolfe and Anatole France," *Comparative Literature,* IX (Winter, 1957), 33-50.

Devoto, Bernard, "Genius Is Not Enough," *Saturday Review of Literature,* XIII (Apr. 25, 1936), 3-4, 14-15, and *Forays and Rebuttals,* Boston: Little, Brown, 1936. Also in *Enigma.* Condemns Wolfe's failure to provide structure and mature idea.

Fagin, N. Bryllion, "In Search of an American Cherry Orchard," *Texas Quarterly,* I (Summer-Autumn, 1958), 132-141.

Foster, Ruel E., "Fabulous Tom Wolfe," *University of Kansas City Review* XXIII (Summer, 1957), 260-264.

Frohock, W. M., "Thomas Wolfe: Of Time and Neurosis," *Southwest Review,* XXXIII (Autumn, 1948), 349-360. Revised for *The Novel of Violence,* Dallas, Texas: University Press. 1950. Also in *Enigma.*

Halperin, Irving, "Torrential Production": Thomas Wolfe's Writing Practices," *Arizona Quarterly,* XIV (1958), 29-34.

.........., "Wolfe's *Of Time and the River*," *Explicator,* XVIII (November, 1959), Item 9.

Holman, C. Hugh, "The Loneliness at the Core," *New Republic,* CXXXIII (October 10, 1955), 16-17.

.........., *Thomas Wolfe* (University of Minnesota Pamphlets on American Writers, No. 6), Minneapolis: University of Minnesota Press, 1960. A general introduction to Wolfe's fiction.

.........., ed., *The World of Thomas Wolfe,* New York: Scribner's, 1962. A research anthology containing selections of essays by Wolfe and his critics, with suggested topics for research.

Johnson, Edgar, "Thomas Wolfe and the American Dream," *A Treasury of **Satire**,* ed. by E. Johnson, New York: Simon and Shuster, 1945.

Johnson, Pamela Hansford, *Hungry Gulliver: An English Critical Appraisal of Thomas Wolfe,* New York and London: Scribner's, 1948. Sees Wolfe as the novelist of young America, the most significant figure in three past decades of American literature. His work, for her, is a unified expression of his quest.

Kennedy, Richard S., *The Window of Memory; The Literary Career of Thomas Wolfe,* Chapel Hill, N.C.: University of North Carolina Press, 1962. A study of Wolfe manuscripts.

Kussy, Bella, "The Vitalist Trend and Thomas Wolfe," *Sewanee Review,* L (July-Sept., 1942), 306-324. Finds in Wolfe the same respect for power and dynamic energy as in Bergson and Nietzsche.

McElderry, Bruce R., Jr., "The Durable Humor in *Look Homeward, Angel,*" *Arizona Quarterly,* XI (Summer, 1955), 123-128.

.........., *Thomas Wolfe,* New York: Twayne Publishers, 1964. A general introduction to Wolfe.

.........., "Thomas Wolfe: Dramatist," *Modern Drama,* VI (May, 1963), 1-11. Adapted as Chapter II of Thomas Wolfe.

Muller, Herbert J., *Thomas Wolfe,* Norfolk, Connecticut: New Directions, 1947. An evaluative and interpretive analysis of Wolfe's attempt to create an American myth.

Natanson, M.A. "Privileged Moment: A Study in the Rhetoric of Thomas Wolfe," *Quarterly Journal of Speech,* XLIII (April, 1957), 143-150.

Reeves, Paschal, "The Humor of Thomas Wolfe." *Southern Folklore Quarterly,* XXIV (June, 1960), 109-120. Wolfe's folk humor.

Rothman, Nathan L., "Thomas Wolfe and James Joyce: A Study in Literary Influence," ed. by Allen Tate, A *Southern Vanguard,* Englewood Cliffs, New Jersey: Prentice-Hall, 1947, pp. 52-77. Also in *Enigma.* A study of Wolfe's handling of Joycean **themes** and of the progress which he was making in acquiring greater objectivity in his later works.

Rubin, Louis D., Jr., *Thomas Wolfe: The Weather of His Youth,* Baton Rouge: Louisiana State University Press, 1955. Critical and thematic analysis of Wolfe in relation to his family and the South.

Schorer, Mark, "Technique as Discovery." *Hudson Review,* I (Spring, 1948), 67-87.

Stearns, Monroe M., "The Metaphysics of Thomas Wolfe," *College English,* VI (January, 1945), 193-199. Also in *Enigma.*

Stevens, Virginia, "Thomas Wolfe's America," *Mainstream,* XI (Jan., 1958), 1-24.

Walser, Richard, ed., *The Enigma of Thomas Wolfe: Biographical and Critical Selections,* Cambridge, Mass.: Harvard University Press, 1953. Collects many of the best articles on Wolfe.

.........., *Thomas Wolfe: An Introduction and Interpretation,* New York: Barnes and Noble, 1961. A general introduction stronger on biography than criticism.

With the exception of the analysis of *Look Homeward, Angel* the treatment of the novels tends to be mere plot summary.

Watkins, Floyd C., "Thomas Wolfe's High Sinfulness of Poetry," *Modern Fiction Studies,* II (Winter, 1956), 197 - 206. Analyzes Wolfes' style.

Wolfe, Thomas, *The Story of a Novel,* New York: Scribner's, 1936. A lecture delivered in July, 1935, revised and published in articles in the *Saturday Review, December,* 1935. An explanation of the process of creation which led to the writing of *Of Time and the River.*

See also the sections of Wolfe in the following.

General Studies

Beach, Joseph Warren, *American Fiction: 1920-1940,* New York; Macmillan, 1941.

Geismar, Maxwell, *Writers in Crisis: The American Novel, 1925-1940*, New York: Macmillan, 1941.

Gelfant, Blanche Housman, *The American City Novel,* Norman, Oklahoma: University of Oklahoma Press, 1954.

Kazin, Alfred, *On Native Grounds: An Interpretation of Modern American Prose Literature*, New York: Reynal and Hitchcock, 1942

Correspondence

Cargill, Oscar, and Thomas Clark Pollock, eds., The *Correspondence of Thomas Wolfe and Homer Andrew Watt,* New York: New York University Press, 1954.

Nowell, Elizabeth, ed., *The Letters of Thomas Wolfe*, New York: Scribner's, 1956.

Terry, John Skally, ed., *Thomas Wolfe's Letters to His Mother,* Julia Elizabeth Wolfe, New York: Scribner's, 1943.

EXPLORE THE ENTIRE LIBRARY OF BRIGHT NOTES STUDY GUIDES

From Shakespeare to Sinclair Lewis and from Plato to Pearl S. Buck, The Bright Notes Study Guide library spans hundreds of volumes, providing clear and comprehensive insights into the world's greatest literature. Discover more, faster with the Bright Notes Study Guide to the classics you're reading today.

STUDY GUIDE TO GREAT EXPECTATIONS BY CHARLES DICKENS

STUDY GUIDE TO THE ROMANTIC POETS BY PETRONIUS

STUDY GUIDE TO BELOVED BY TONI MORRISON

STUDY GUIDE TO ROMEO AND JULIET BY WILLIAM SHAKESPEARE

STUDY GUIDE TO WUTHERING HEIGHTS BY EMILY BRONTË

See the entire library of available
Bright Notes guides at **BrightNotes.com**

Available in print and digital wherever books are sold

INFLUENCE PUBLISHERS

9 781645 425021